Embracing The Moon

BOOKS BY

KEN STANGE

Love Is A Grave (Nebula Press)

Bushed (York Publishing)

Nocturnal Rhythms (Penumbra Press)

These Proses A Problem Or Two (Two Cultures Press)

Cold Pigging Poetics (York Publishing)

More Than Ample (Two Cultures Press)

Bourgeois Pleasures (Quarry Press)

Colonization Of a Cold Planet (Two Cultures Press)

Advice To Travellers (Penumbra Press)

A Smoother Pebble, A Prettier Shell (Penumbra Press)

The Sad Science Of Love (Two Cultures Press)

God When He's Drunk (Two Cultures Press)

Embracing The Moon

Twenty-Five Little Worlds

Ken Stange

For information about permission to reprint, record, or perform sections of this book, write to Two Cultures Press, 970 Copeland, North Bay, Ontario, Canada, P1B 3E4 (info@twoculturespress.com)

Library and Archives Canada Cataloguing in Publication

Stange, Ken, 1946-, author   Embracing the moon : (twenty-five little worlds) / Ken Stange.

Summary: A collection of digital art works paired with tanka poems.ISBN 978-0-9809273-7-5 (pbk.)

     1. Waka, Canadian (English). I. Title. II. Title: Twenty-five little worlds.

PS8587.T3E43 2013   C811'.54   C2013-907604-2

Acknowledgements

"Herbalist's World" appeared in *The League of Canadian Poets Blog* (April, 2009)

Thanks to Claudia Coutu Radmore for permission to reprint her tanka that originally appeared in *Gusts* (#4, 2006)

The great Chinese poet, Li Po for inspiration. The title alludes to the legend that he died by drowning when—having consumed too much wine—he leaned out from his boat to embrace the reflection of the moon in the still water.

Cover Design: Ken Stange

ISBN: 978-0-9809273-7-5

For **Ursula**

CONTENTS

"Less is indeed more. The image on the retina or on the page that flickers and is gone is the one that lives on in memory."
                                                                    —Hippokrites

a bat or night bird
flies across my field of vision
a dark slash
between this moment
and this moment

                              —Claudia Coutu Radmore (in *Gusts #4, 2006*)

The Tanka Welcomed To Our Shores

Polonius had it right: Brevity *is* the soul of wit. Yes, of course, even the garrulous has its place, for to everything there is a literary form. But it is the scalpel that sharpens most writing. Rarely do excisions damage the body of any literary creation. Usually they just remove imperfections, perhaps benign but still unsightly growths. Writing is easy, but editing is difficult—for editing entails wielding the scalpel. This is why the strictures of structured verse so often have produced the best poems. The writer when putting on the editor's hat is also donning the surgeon's gown. And a good surgeon needs to practice his sullen craft, keep his scalpel sharpened. There is no better place to do this than within such incredibly constricted and succinct poetic forms as the tanka.

.

The tanka, like the haiku, is originally a Japanese verse form. Obviously Japanese is a very different language from English, and translation of Japanese poetry into English presents even more difficulties than are always and inevitably present, especially in terms of prosody. The best translators, such as Kenneth Rexroth and Arthur Waley, concentrated on the spirit of the poetic form rather than trying to strictly adhere to some approximation of the formal structure. The Japanese language is not accentual, and so like French (and unlike English or the Germanic languages) its formal verse forms are based on counting syllables, not accents. But it is even worse when it comes to Japanese, for what linguists called an "*on*" is not strictly speaking equivalent to the English syllable.

.

Nevertheless, two traditional Japanese poetic forms were 'translated' into English forms in the late Nineteenth Century by the writer Masaoka Shiki. They are *haiku* (originally called *hokku*) and *tanka* (a subcategory of *waka*). He made the structural transformation from what were originally one long line (sometimes vertical) poems in these two forms into English poetic structures of three and five lines, respectively, with a set number of syllables per line. For haikus it was 5/7/5; and for tankas it was 5/7/5/7/7. This roughly approximates the short/long sound unit structure of the Japanese forms.

.

For some reason this imported structure caught on, and with the rise of the Imagist movement became entrenched as an English poetic form. Unlike some of the other imports (such as the French and Italian, which when strictly adhered to require straining for repeated rhymes and meeting prosodic requirements far easier in their original language), haiku and tanka are 'easy'. All one has to do is count syllables and be succinct. There is no need to balance accented and unaccented syllables or concern oneself with end rhymes or any of the other paraphernalia associated with most formal poetic structures. You needn't know a dactyl from a pterodactyl, an anapest from a pest; and so you needn't worry about shooting yourself in your metric foot when writing a haiku or a tanka. All you had to be able to do was recognize a syllable when it bit you on the tongue—and know how to count! It was a verse form made to order for the amateur who wanted the status of writing something other than "free verse".

Unfortunately, like with free verse, doing it well was not really that easy. Good so-called "free" verse, like jazz, is far from free, is actually extremely intricate and complicated. For a composer, declining to employ such structures as sonata allegro form does not mean that anything goes—or works. And so in poetry, while haiku and tanka may dispense with a lot of constraints, they strictly apply one of the most demanding constraints of all: succinctness.

It just ain't that easy to pack a lot of meaning into seventeen, or even thirty-one, English syllables. While it is true that since the *on* is a sound unit that is often shorter than the equivalent English syllable, and so the English haiku or tanka is actually longer than its Japanese equivalent, English does not have as many words that carry complex and established associations and allusions as Japanese. So-called "pillow words" with their standardized associations are an example of this, as are all the Japanese words that have multiple, sometimes punning, meanings and connotations. Japanese can pack more punch per word than English.

For this reason, good and genuinely affecting, resonant English haiku and tanka are rare, despite the ever increasing number of writers attempting them. This is not to say there aren't some wonderful English haiku and tankas—or imagist poems (based on the idea of—if not strict adherence to—the form). The imagist poems of William Carlos Williams (e.g., "The Red Wheelbarrow) and Ezra Pound (e.g., "In A Station Of The Metro") spring to mind. And there are numerous literary journals that consistently publish first-rate haiku and tanka. But the former is the harder task-master and definitely is less acclimatized to an English language environment.

The tanka is just tight enough to be demanding, but with enough room for the oversized occidental to move about naturally. It is the perfect exercise room for a poet who wishes to concentrate on tone and definition, not bulk. Whether one wishes to invoke further restraints such as avoiding rhymes, or allow extensions such as not always sticking to the precise 5/7/5/7/7 format, just wrestling with tankas is rewarding. It is one of the most successfully integrated and assimilated immigrants to the English poetic world. I suspect that eventually it will, like the sonnet, assume a major place in the standard prosodic repertoire. It certainly should.

These Tankas And Their Little Worlds

I am a writer first and a visual artist second. When I began to create images with tools other than words, I set myself the artistic constraint of always integrating textual components with my images. It seemed right and proper homage to my origins.

.

Rarely, however, have I felt the text in my artworks to have much validity as an independent unit, for often it was merely a few words or phrases. And even when it was more than that, and I did feel it was a bit closer to achieving poetic status, I still felt it owed its meaningful existence to its relationship to the visual image, which was what I considered paramount, its *raison d'être*.

.

However, in my artwork series entitled "Tanka Spheres" on which this book is based, I deviated from this usual relationship of the words to the text. I chose the tanka as the vehicle for this experiment because of its succinct nature. I felt any longer poetic form would overwhelm the image.

.

However, the tankas in this book are not conventional tankas (although they all rigorously conform to the 5/7/5/7/7 syllabic convention), because they are wedded to the accompanying image. They differ from conventional tankas in the same way that song lyrics differ from poems; that is to say, the words are intended to cohabit with another art form, and like any really compatible couple, create a whole greater than the parts. These words, however, are mated with images not sounds.

.

Even brilliant song lyrics when removed from their musical context often lie dead on the page. But although one doesn't really expect them to stand alone, sometimes they do. I believe this also is true of these poems. I can see some of them having some life on their own, although I still believe they are enhanced by their visual partners. Others may, I fear, seem incomprehensible, obscure, and inanimate without their visual mate to prop them up.

.

Songwriters are routinely asked which came first, the lyrics or the tune. While for many songwriters this seems an annoying chicken and egg type of question, I can say unequivocally that for these works of mine, it was the image that came first. I hatched the image and then cracked it open to see what words came stumbling out.

.

In the actual artworks, I put the words (all tankas) side by side with the images. I intended this to elevate the text to equal status with the visual image—a status, as I've just said, I never before felt text had achieved in my art. In this book, in this spirit of equality, I've split the original work, placing image and text verso recto.

.

The actual original artworks from "Tanka Spheres" look like this.

C95: Tanka Spheres - Bather's World

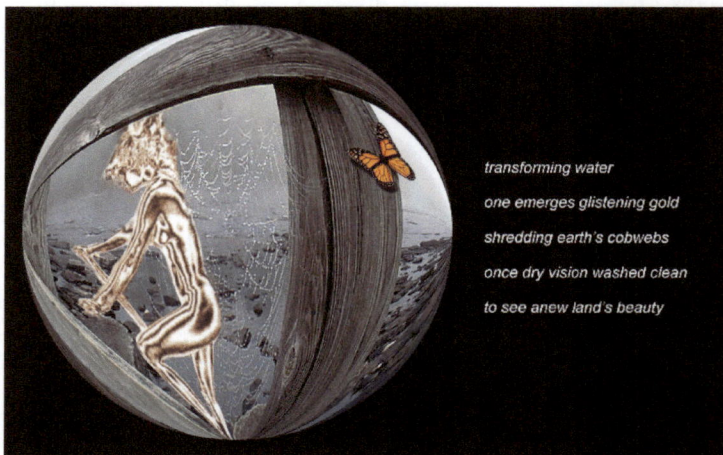

transforming water
one emerges glistening gold
shredding earth's cobwebs
once dry vision washed clean
to see anew land's beauty

Ken Stange

The images, like the verses, stick to a strict formal format. They are all spherized images of digital artworks, which were originally conventional rectangular images. All are based on the visual theme of a glass globe containing a world—much like those glass globes sold at Christmas with kitschy winter scenes that fill with snow when one shakes them. It is a wonderful coincidence that the number of syllables in a tanka is 31 and pi rounded is 3.1. But then both art and science are about mathematical 'coincidences', about order, about balance. I sincerely hope these works achieve a true balance between the word and the image.

.

Finally I have to shame-facedly admit I have appended notes on all of the poems. I do this partially because English has few "pillow words", and I cannot blithely assume the reader will share the rich connotations associated in my mind with all of the key words in these poems. I do it also because there is pleasure in talking about the underlying inspiration.

.

Frankly I'm uncomfortable with this, for it seems much like explaining a joke—which of course never really carries the humour. But my hope is that when in most cases these notes merely seem obvious and unnecessary explications, the reader will forgive my condescension in appending them. *And also* I'd like to believe that sometimes the wee bit of background to my inspiration they give will be found to be of interest—and perhaps even slightly enrich the poem.

The 25 Little Worlds

Bather's World

transforming water

one emerges glistening gold

shredding earth's cobwebs

once dry vision washed clean

to see anew land's beauty

Benoit's World

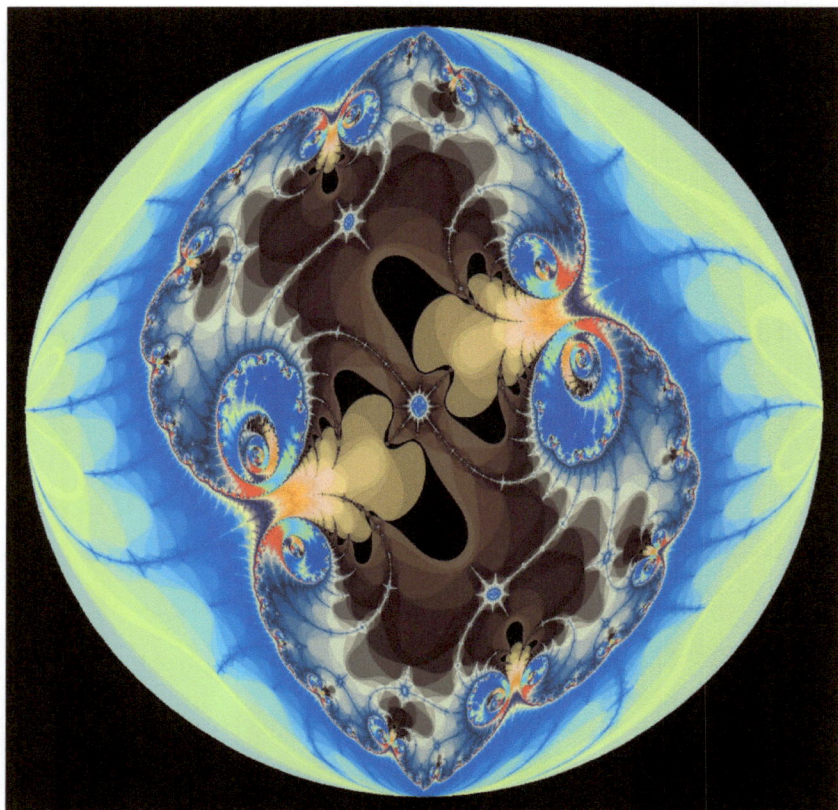

such beauty in math

where all shorelines have no length

such beauty in graphs

where iteration is king

and magnification rules

Bird's World

birds in glass cages

a well rounded world vision

a sphere with a view

observation reflection

outside and inside combined

Boatman'sWorld

we all long to sail

the head waters of the Styx

aboard Ra's sky boat

go to there where dragons be

skimming billows slay the night

Boneman'sWorld

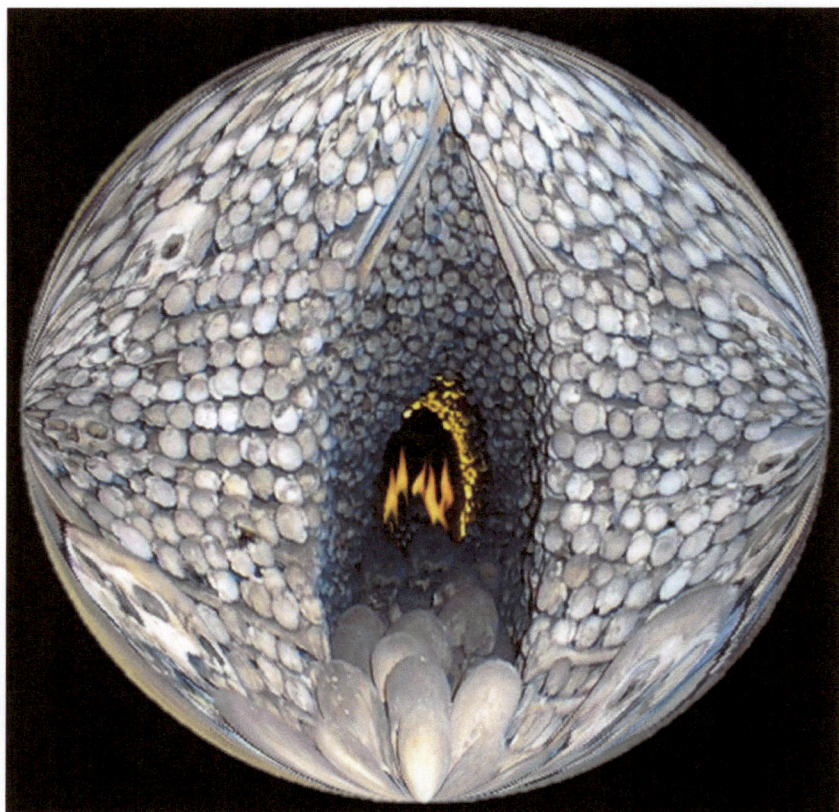

down in ancient caves

fire burned on the cold cold stone

were ancestral bones

the weapons used in those hunts

which fed them and led to us?

Butterfly's World

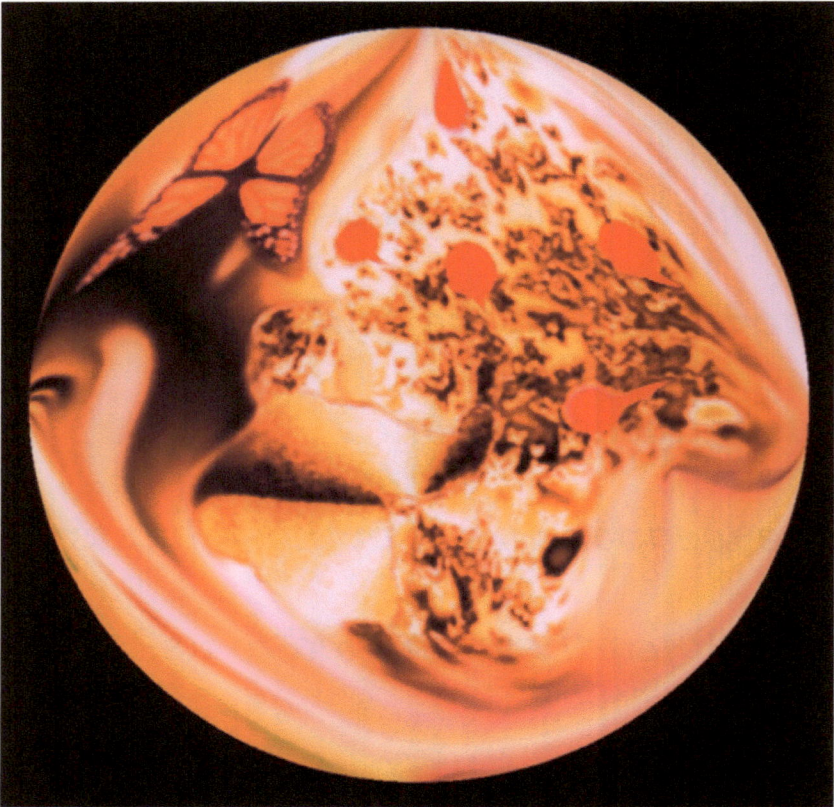

moving through three worlds

larva, pupa, butterfly

inseminator

wearing warning toxic orange

at last aptly crowned monarch

Calder's World

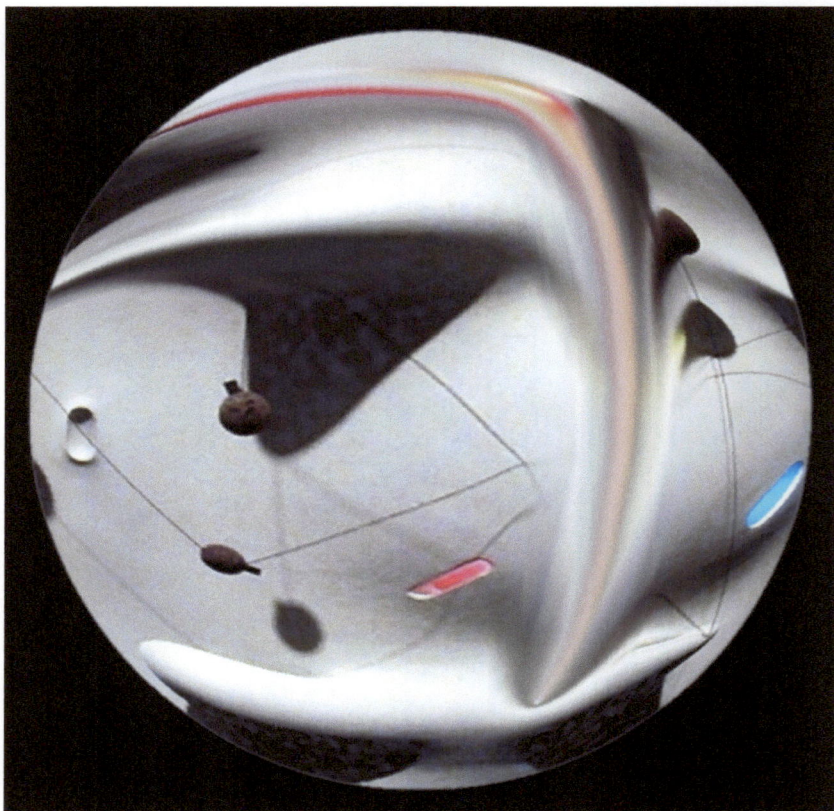

erratic orbits

improbably sweet shapes

drunken astrolabe

staid perception made mobile

blowing in the cosmic wind

Farmer's World

magic for us all

to drop seed and learn patience

claim credit for life

there's no greater gift than this

dirt beneath our fingernails

Flow's World

into river step

let time's arrow pierce you deep

let life's blood flow out

join the stream that carries all

down to destination death

Goldman's World

nothing gold can stay

sundown colour of the seas

rare nobility

rich glow of autumnal trees

even frost lights gold's display

Hatchling's World

small safety is nest

does not compare to egg's world

outside is scary

why crack one's white firmament

heaven ain't beyond that shell

Herbalist's World

life's garden demands

parsley sage rosemary thyme

our salad days' needs

too bland be our daily meal

without season's seasonings

Hermaphrodite's World

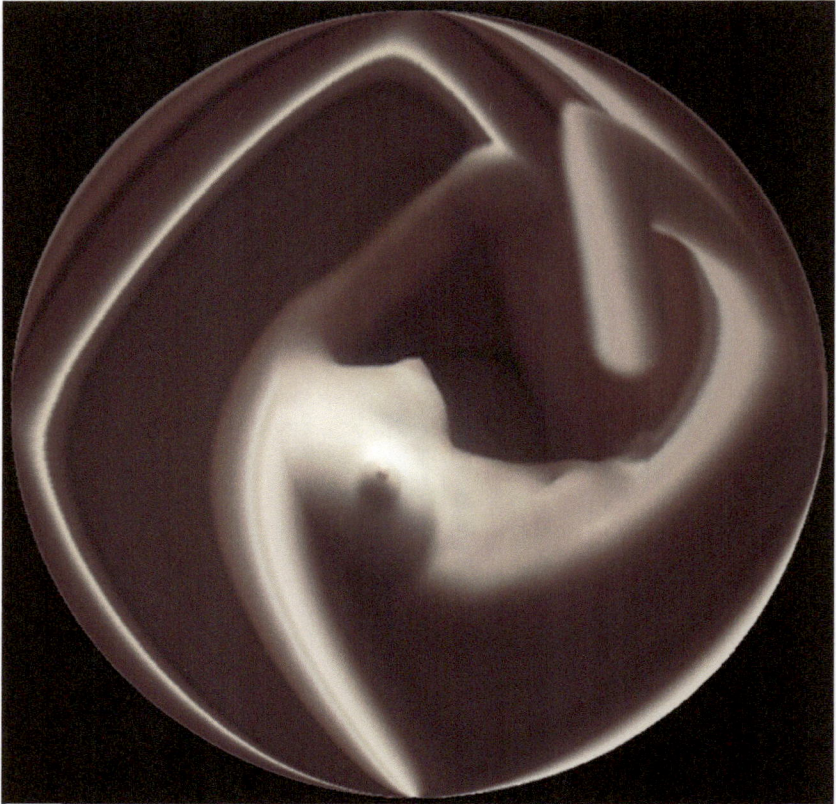

recursive loving

our age of androgyny

hermaphrodite is

narcissism's fulfillment

ability to love oneself

Hunter's World

when the bridge branches

the deer like the hunter pauses

there is no right choice

just possible consensus

one wants but other does not

Iguana's World

rare time traveller

mesozoic survivor

lasting reminder

of nature's profligacy

all creatures' fragility

Julia's World

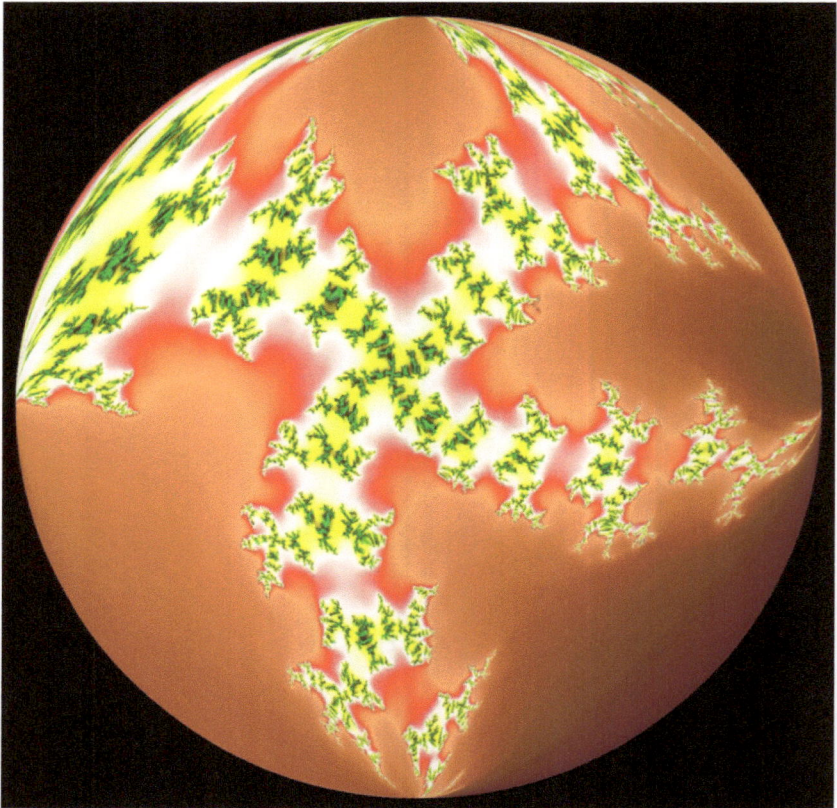

math's micro islands

magic archipelagos

minute differences

in initial directions

map very different worlds

Lover's World

the warrior knows

sometimes love ain't so easy

his lover knows too

nature's armour does protect

yet best is unprotected

Medievalist's World

go to past's haven

relive pageantry and pomp

see with eyes wide shut

glory in naiveté

drink and blindly be merry

Northerner's World

unclothed limbs stretching

still water wrapped in white sheets

cool naked beauty

welcome azure dappled sky

peace that comes in winter's pause

Rebel's World

torn double agent

loyalty versus freedom

cold war versus peace

the patriot found guilty

but the rebel crucified

Symbiote's World

all life is tangled

just as all bad contains good

woodpecker serves tree

so reciprocating tree

offers nest drum dinner plate

Talisman's World

trust an amulet

magic sphere above our hearts

small world of comfort

we need false securities

or we'd dare not move about

Urbanite's World

glass canyons steel-framed

a thousand windows watching

second-hand sunlight

reflections and refractions

smoothing edges and angles

Waterboy's World

island as refuge

fountain as deep as the sea

forever ripples

sound of water drizzling down

recurrent currents so blue

Weaver's World

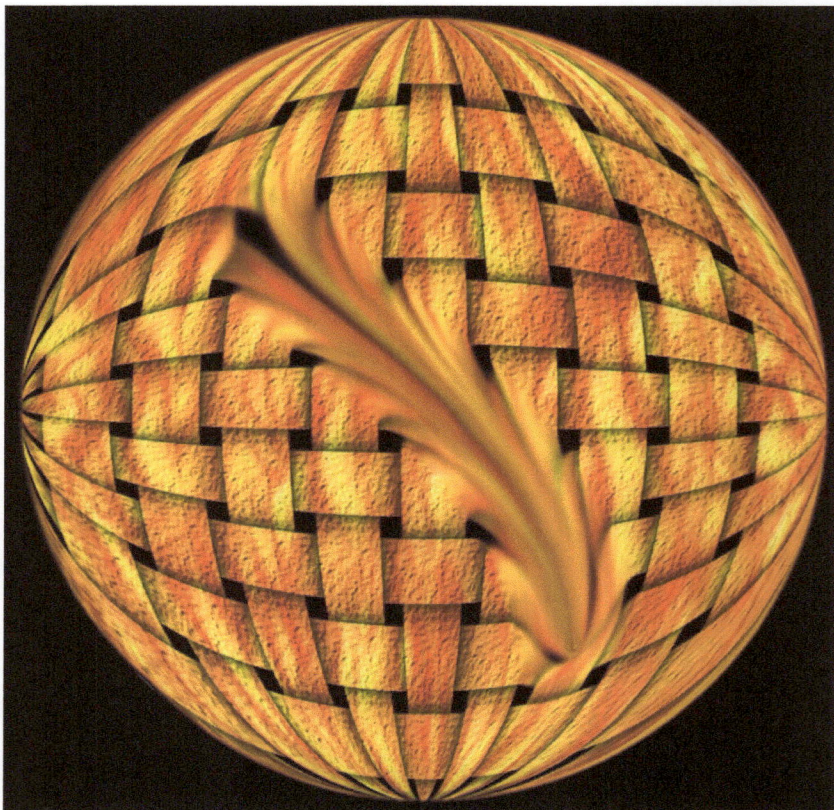

pattern reassures

deviation refreshes

balance makes good art

cross warp with weft yin with yang

weave your world but drop a stitch

Notes on Poems

Bather's World
Immersion in water and resurfacing with cleansed soul and senses is a universal symbol. Ablution equals absolution in the baptism. On the secular level, as the water slides from our bodies it takes with it all the grime on the lenses with which we view the world.

.

Benoit's World
Benoit is a reference to Benoit Mandelbrot, author of *The Fractal Geometry of Nature,* and the person most credited with making the wonderful world of fractal geometry of great interest to mathematicians and artists alike. A fractal image is basically a mathematical graph of repeated iterations of a simple formula. What is interesting to artists about the image/graph so produced is the beauty of its just-less-than-perfect iterative symmetry. (Of course the beauty of these images depends on the effective setting and linking of colour parameters to mathematical ones—and is not always successful.) What is interesting to mathematicians is that fractals are non-integer geometrical units. This is most commonly explained by pointing out that the length of the shoreline of an island depends on the degree of magnification..

.

Bird's World
The bird in the cage is often used as metaphor for a restricted and restrained world. But really all our worlds are limited, spherical domains from which we try to look out and beyond, and what we see is distorted—and probably, should we escape, be found hostile.

.

Boatman's World
According to Egyptian mythology the god Ra represents the sun, and every day he sails the heavens in a sky boat which dips below the horizon at dusk and enters a dark place where live dragons—but emerges unscathed each dawn. Mixing mythologies and metaphors, Styx is the dark river in Greek mythology that separates the land of the living from Hades, the land of the dead.

.

Boneman's World
The images of bones used to create the art are based on photographs taken in the ossuary of the Cemetery Church of All Saints, located on the outskirts of Kutná Hora in the Czech Republic. The ossuary contains the skeletal remains of at least 40,000 people, mostly victims of the 14th century plague years. During construction of the chapel, these bones were unearthed

and, according to legend, a half-blind monk took on the task of stacking them in the chapel. In 1870 a Czech wood-carver, František Rint, arranged them artistically. (Many were used to create bells in the four corners of the chapel.) The macabre beauty of this ossuary has to remind one of the irony inherent in death being a beautiful gift to each new generation.

.

Butterfly's World
The Monarch Butterfly's beautiful and striking orange coloration is a warning to would-be predators that this royal creature would be a foul-tasting and poisonous meal. The mature royal Monarch—selfless distributor of seed for so many other lovely species in the botanical kingdom—had armed himself as an infant (in its larval or caterpillar stage) by taking as his milk that of the milkweed—which contains the toxic cardenolide aglycones. Long live the King!

.

Calder's World
Alexander Calder (avant-garde artist and friend of Jean Arp, Joan Miró, and Marcel Duchamp) invented the mobile, which like so many of the at-the-time radical artistic conceptions has since been widely embraced and even become commonplace: Mobiles now hang over millions of cribs. Their unpredictable movement as air currents affect them are as mysterious and fascinating as the movement of the celestial spheres must have been before Copernicus and Newton. The image that is the basis for this artwork is based on a photograph of a Calder mobile at the Hirshhorn Museum in Washington, D.C.

.

Farmer's World
This work is not just about the farmer, but rather about everyone who discovers the magic and sense of empowerment one gets from pushing a tiny seed into rich, dark earth and then watching it break through the soil, reach for the sun, and eventually offer up to the sower something beautiful to satisfy that most fundamental of all human needs: sustenance.

.

Flow's World
The reference here is to the pre-Socratic philosopher Heraclitus' famous aphorism that no man steps into the same river twice. And time, like a river, is unidirectional.

.

Goldman's World
The first line of this tanka is a quotation of the last line from Robert Frost's famous poem of the same title, and the last line embeds a respectful pun and homage to the poet. Gold is considered a "noble" metal because it does not easily oxidize or tarnish—and of course its physical, spatial scarcity is an echo of its temporal, transient scarcity which is key to its value.

.

Hatchling's World

One summer we noticed a vireo repeatedly visiting the dense interior of an apple tree whose branches hung over our rear deck. It took very close examination to discover a well camouflaged nest with four tiny eggs. Almost every day (when Ma was away) I photographed the nest. The eggs gave forth hatchlings, and the hatchlings became fledglings, and eventually the nest became vacant. Rather than cliché thoughts about "the security of the nest" what struck me was that the nest actually represented an increase in vulnerability. Our comfort and security decreases with each stage of our lives.

Herbalist's World

Simon and Garfunkel made the refrain "parsley, sage, rosemary and thyme" famous with their 1966 album of the same name, but the precise refrain dates back at least to 18th Century versions of a famous medieval ballad. There is wonderful symbolism dating back to the Middle Ages associated with these herbs. Parsley was said to remove bitterness. Sage symbolized strength. Rosemary represented faithfulness. Thyme symbolized courage. Life would indeed be bland without these virtues to season it.

Hermaphrodite's World

Love of self has come to be praised rather than condemned as narcissistic. And 'self-esteem', with or without any justification in real accomplishment, is now considered a virtue. From this it would seem to follow that soon the expression "Go fuck yourself!" will lose its negative implications.

Hunter's World

The hunter and the hunted have a strange relationship in that, unlike in human relationships, thinking alike benefits only one of the parties and actually leads to the demise of the other.

Iguana's World

Reptiles evolved from amphibians 250 millions years ago and eventually became the dominant fauna during was has been called "The Age of Reptiles" (the Mesozoic Period). However, few reptiles survived the Permian Extinction which wiped out 95% of the existing species. By the beginning of the Cenozoic Period, beginning 65 million years ago, reptiles had been replaced by mammals. Now there are a mere 6,000 species of reptiles remaining. Saurians are not of our time and seem to be here just to teach us a painful lesson in natural history.

Julia's World

The image that is spherically mapped here is a colour graph created by playing with a math formula for the Julia set. In mathematics, the Julia set is related to the Mandelbrot Set. As is typical of fractals, the smallest deviation in one parameter of the original generative formula results in dramatically different outcomes after iteration. In plain language, this means that small changes in initial conditions lead to dramatic differences in the end result. The famous example of this principle is the saying (based on a seminal paper by Edward Lorenz on Chaos Theory) that the flapping of a butterfly's wings in Brazil can result in a tornado in Texas. A simple, primary quadratic function that produces such diverse results is to take a number squared plus some arbitrary value (often symbolized by c) and repeat the calculation. If this arbitrary value c includes i (the square root of negative one) truly wonderful things happen.

$$f_c(z) = z^2 + c$$

Lover's World

When visiting the Roger Williams Zoo in Providence, Rhode Island, I happened to catch two African Spurred Tortoises mating. Obviously no less amorous for their protective armour, they rocked slowly and laboriously back and forth. Such a sight inevitably makes one chuckle and snicker, for there is something inherently ludicrous about the copulatory act in all species. But it also makes one think about vulnerability. Lovers are always vulnerable, but the best loving occurs when one is most vulnerable.

Medievalist's World

It seems to me that passionate historians come in two primary shades: bright or dark. Some see the past as glorious and locate the Golden Age at some time long gone. Others see the past as an age of darkness and ignorance and take it as a lesson in what to avoid in the future. Inevitably the former have to cast a blind eye on that which the latter focuses. The line in the poem "see with eyes wide shut" alludes to the title of Kubrick's last film which has been interpreted as referring to the innocent wide-eyed view of things that does not really allow one to see what is actually there.

Northerner's World

The image here is based on a photograph I took one morning of a spot along a trail beside Lake Nipissing in Northern Ontario and a few blocks from my house. Visible on the horizon are the Manitou Islands, five miles from shore. For over six years every morning I have walked this trail with my dog Nick, no matter the season or the weather. Always a welcome contemplative pause at the beginning of my day, there is a special, deep stillness on those minus 20 winter mornings when the air achieves a clarity never to be found in the south—and rarely in my mind.

Rebel's World

Interestingly, the photograph from which this artwork was created was taken in Washington, D.C. We'd just visited the Viet Nam War memorial and the book I'd taken along for our trip was the spy novel *Tinker, Tailor, Soldier, Spy* by John le Carré.

Symbiote's World
Symbiosis (the scientific term for a reciprocal, mutually beneficial relationship between different species) is the glue that binds an ecosystem into a coherent harmonious whole. Woodpeckers eat wood borers, bark lice and other insects harmful to trees. In return trees serve as the bird's dinner plate and offer their real estate for the nests—room and board, so to speak. Furthermore, the tree is the percussive musical instrument on which the woodpecker taps out a tune to woo his mate.

Talisman's World
A talisman or amulet is commonly worn around the neck, symbolically hanging over the heart, in the belief it will ward off evil and misfortune. What is interesting is these amulets often are very sinister in appearance. Balls of concentric blue and white circles representing an evil eye are a common apotropaic talisman worn by Turks and other peoples of the Middle East. Even the common cross worn by Christians is really sinister, if one thinks about it, for the crucifix is an instrument of torture. Consistent with this, I've created a talisman image that appears more malevolent than reassuring.

Urbanite's World
The canyons of an urban centre share more with those of the natural world than is generally acknowledged or appreciated and have a special kind of beauty. In fact, sunlight often more easily penetrates these urban canyons than it does those of the natural world, for it is reflected and refracted down by the glass walls of the city canyons. This artwork is based on a particularly reflective piece of architecture: the new addition to Toronto's Royal Ontario Museum.

Waterboy's World
While no man *is* an island, every man *wants* an island. An island symbolizes a stable and secure place, an unchanging refuge from the deteriorating mainland. I'm sure the fascination with rafts or boats and fountains reflects this. (The boy in the image was sitting on one of the tiny 'islands' in a fountain at the SUNY campus in Albany, New York.)

Weaver's World
This shamelessly didactic poem is an expression of an essential tenet of my aesthetic. The best art satisfies and balances both our need for order and our desire for tension and surprise. The most satisfying existence does the same, but it is more attainable in art than in life.

Author's Note

Literature, like science, is a way of exploring different perspectives. The results of these literary explorations, like the results of science, are always inherently tentative. It is for this reason that I choose to call my books *hypotheses*. ***Embracing The Moon: 25 Little Worlds***, completed June 20, 2008, is *Hypothesis 16*.

Website: *KenStange.com*
Other books available at *TwoCulturesPress.com*